M000018087

# 101 things to know before you date my daughter, my best friend, or me.

# 101 Things to Know Before you Date my daughter, my best friend, or me

*Written by*
*One of LA's most celebrated Radio Personalities*

## JOSEFA SALINAS

BLUE DOLPHIN

Copyright © 2005 Josefa Salinas
All Rights Reserved.
www.101thingstoknow.com

Published by Blue Dolphin Publishing, Inc.
P.O. Box 8, Nevada City, CA 95959
Orders: 1 800 643-0765
Web: www.bluedolphinpublishing.com

ISBN: 1-57733-165-6

Library of Congress Cataloging-in-Publication Data

Salinas, Josefa.
    101 things to know before you date my daughter, my best friend, or me /
Josefa Salinas.
       p. cm.
    ISBN 1-57733-165-6 (pbk. : alk. paper)
    1. Dating (Social customs)—Miscellanea. 2. Man-woman
relationships—Miscellanea. I. Title: One hundred one things to know
before you date my daughter, my best friend, or me. II. Title: One hundred
and one things to know before you date my daughter, my best friend, or
me. III. Title.

    HQ801.S425 2005
    306.73—dc22

                                                                            2005005010

Teen-Adult Non-fiction        Singles & Married Couples
Radio Personalities           Hispanic Authors
Health Education

Please look for upcoming children's series "Cool Adventures" and other
fine works by radio personality and author, Josefa Salinas.

Cover Design: Annabel Layug, annabellayug@hotmail.com

First Printing, April, 2005

To purchase books at volume discount, please contact the publisher
directly. Special discount rates available for charities and qualified
organizations. For celebrity appearances and media interviews, contact
staff through the book's web site listed above. Information will be routed
to proper staff.

Printed in the United States of America
by Delta Printing Solutions, Valencia CA

Purchase of this book also supports multiple local charities.

10   9   8   7   6   5   4   3   2   1

## TO MY DAUGHTER PARESS

If there is a way I could have all your heartaches for you, I would. Do you remember your first broken heart? I remember telling you everything would be okay and I was sorry to say it probably would not be the last time you felt this way. My wish is that you read this book and learn from the mistakes and blessings of many who have walked the road before you. Perhaps it will save you a wrong turn down this winding road of love. Men are the most exciting, wonderful, frustrating creatures you will ever experience. Know that you are never alone on the journey. I will always be by your side, supporting you through good times and bad. You have the tools, now go out there and enjoy the wonderful adventure of life and love.

## TO MY DAUGHTERS: ARTISHA, BRANDI, JACKIE, DAWNY, SHELLY, SIMIE, TREISHA, JEANNAE, CRISTAL AND SARA

Although I did not give birth to you myself, I couldn't love you more. I will always be here for you.

TO MY DEAREST FRIENDS: ZELYKA, SHARON,
IRIS, DREA, MARIANNE, MAUREEN, KIMMIE,
GWEN, DIANNA, MARGIE AND AUNTIE PAULA

Thanks for always being there no matter what guy was in our lives.

TO THE MEN WHO HAVE COME AND GONE
IN MY LIFE : THANKS FOR THE HEARTACHE,
TEARS, JOY, PAIN, LAUGHTER, FRUSTRATION,
AGONY AND ECSTASY

Without it all, I would not be the woman I am today.

A special thanks, acknowledgment and blessing to Yvonne at Begining2End in Nevada. Because of you, my dream has come to life.

# PREFACE

I have spent the last twenty years working in the broadcast industry as an air personality and community advocate. In Los Angeles at Power 106, I helped create "The Slo Jam Show" where I was known as the "Angelita de la Noche" (angel of the night). Listeners would call me with their most intimate problems and triumphs, and I became acutely aware of the importance of giving sound advice. Whether it was KKSF, KBLX, KJLH, KACE or HOT 92 JAMZ, I have spoken with thousands of people over the last two decades and realized that, from 8 to 80, I had heard it all. Throughout the years, one common theme rang true: No matter what age, ethnic group, economic status or gender, people pretty much had the same complaints and praises for the opposite sex. I have learned so much from my listeners and I thank them from the bottom of my heart.

Being a single mom raising a daughter alone, I wondered how I was going to prepare her for the world of dating and men. I began to write down ideas for the men she would potentially date to help her be the best woman she could be. As I look ahead for my son, I am confident that this book will help him with the women that will be in his life in years to come.

My desire was to write a book that both men and women would enjoy. I may not have all the answers, but I have years of experience being a woman, coupled with thousands and thousands of phone calls from love-sick and happy people to base my findings. I hope you find one or two that mean something to you. You may want to highlight a few passages or leave a comment in the personal note space and then leave the book around for that special someone to find. Whatever you choose, I wish you all the best in love and life.

Josefa
Tu Angelita

# More Critical Acclaim on 101 Things to Know…

"Congratulations on your book!! All the stations you've worked at…I know you must have figured out a thang or two about relationships…I'd give the book to my son or daughter. I'd even read it for myself!"
**- Coolio**

"101 Things is the roadmap that navigates you thru the trials and tribulations of bringing children into the real world. It puts you on the highway to healthy relationships and keeps you there, not only with your kids, but your spouse as well. 101 Things is a must read for parents and teens alike"
**- Rick and Becky Nuhn**

" I have had the honor and pleasure of knowing Josefa Salinas even before she was involved in radio. She's always been ahead of the game in everything she does. Congratulations on your book! As usual Josefa…you go get em' girl!"
**– Howard Hewett**

"This book is truly epignosis (the accurate, precise information) on how to touch the heart of the relationship you desire to maintain and cultivate into something that will last a lifetime and even throughout eternity. This book will indeed affect the lives of those who seek to have a model relationship, one that the world would appreciate. Good job Josefa. I know there is more to come. Thank God for giving you to us in our generation."
**-Dr. Edward Turner, Power of Love Church**

# 101 things to know
## before you date
# my daughter,
# my best friend,
### or me.

101 THINGS TO KNOW BEFORE YOU DATE . . .

## Personal Notes

promise

# ** 1 **

Always call when you say you are going to call. This may sound simple and trivial, but 17 years and thousands of women have confirmed this is their number one complaint about men.

## For the female:

This is the hardest thing to teach a guy. Once he masters this, you'll have someone special. When he calls, call him back. If you're not interested, be kind but tell him.

# Personal Notes

## ** 2 **

Don't lie. It's boring and a waste of time. Women have a sixth sense that is better than a lie detector. We may not always tell you that we know you're lying, but believe me, we know it.

## For the female:
If you find out he is lying to you, it's time to make a choice. Is this something you want to put up with? What if he lies about really important stuff that could mean your life or death? Are you willing to risk it? Most of all, don't be a liar either. It's so much easier to start from a point of truth and a solid foundation than having to look over your shoulder from day to day. The truth could hurt, but a lie can kill you.

# Personal Notes

intuition

## ** 3 **

Out of the blue, and for no reason at all, bring her something unusual with a note attached. If you find it difficult to write, the gift alone will do. Something unique to your day… a shell from the beach, a feather from a bird that reminds you of the softness of her skin, a snow globe of a place she dreams of going. Sound silly? Women are funny like that. We like things that are unique for us alone. Something you took the time to bring that says you were thinking of her will win her heart.

## For the female:

Take a moment to look at what he has brought you. Anyone can buy a dozen roses. A beautiful rock, that glistens in the sunlight, that reminds him of the sparkle in your eye, can't be duplicated.

# Personal Notes

sincerity

## ** 4 **

Catch her eye from across a crowded room. Hold it for a long time even if she turns away. Don't let anything or anyone distract you for at least 30 seconds. No words, no movement, just eyes. You'll be amazed at the results.

## For the female:

If you find the eyes of someone you care for looking at you, look back. Composers of music and verse wish they could capture what transpires in those precious moments when your eyes are locked with someone you desire.

# Personal Notes

## ** 5 **

If your female friends are really "just friends," introduce them to her.

## For the female:

Watch out for this one. The casual phrase "Oh, she's just a friend" is a favorite amongst men. Anyone who is a "friend" should act like one. If you're never invited when "they" get together, this is a problem waiting to happen. Don't go for the old line "she and I were friends for years...you're just going to have to get used to it." If she is really just a "friend," she'll want to include you too. Watch how she acts around the two of you. The eye contact, the comfort level. This will not be hard to figure out. If he won't change his position about the "friend," get rid of the guy.

# Personal Notes

celebration

## ** 6 **

Send her a card in the mail for no reason. Everyone loves to get something special in the mail that doesn't require a return payment.

## For the female:

Remember that this works both ways. Don't forget to acknowledge the things he does for you, and most of all never take them for granted.

# Personal Notes

## ** 7 **

Take her to the park to swing. Push her for as long as you can. Let her be a little girl when she wants to. All women have a little girl inside of them that, when allowed to emerge, will bring lasting smiles to your face.

## For the female:

Let him push you on the swing. Don't be afraid to be that little girl inside. It is what completes you as a woman.

# Personal Notes

peace

# ** 8 **

Take her to the beach, park, or any natural quiet place at sunset. Places like this are featured in magazines and cards around the world to represent a multitude of emotions. The cost is free. The result, priceless.

## For the female:

Remember all those quiet moments spent at sunset. It's amazing how incredible silence can be at that moment. So many thoughts fill your heart. Words are seldom needed. But if he feels like talking, let him. This could be his moment of inspiration to open up and tell you something special. Listen.

# Personal Notes

# ** 9 **

Hold her hand when she least expects it. Like around the guys. Make sure you note her reaction to this. If she doesn't let you hold her hand, better find out why and fast.

## For the female:

Hold his hand back. If he never holds your hand except when you are alone, find out why. This could be a major sign to look for with regard to his desire or ability to show emotion or the truth about his personal status.

## Personal Notes

enrapture

# ** 10 **

Cook her dinner. Or at least invite her over for a dinner that you went out and bought. Find out early on if she can cook. Don't believe that just because she is a woman, she can cook. If this is important to you, it would be a good idea to know from the beginning.

## For the female

Unless it is burned beyond taste, try the cooking. You may be surprised. Most of all you should respect the gesture being presented. If you can't cook, take a class. Everyone should know how to do the basics - MEN AND WOMEN.

# Personal Notes

tranquility

# ** 11 **

Paint her toenails. Sounds simple, but the results are amazing.

## For the female
Make sure he has all the tools and let him paint them any color he likes. Explain the basics and let him go for it. Sit back and close your eyes. It doesn't get much better than this.

# Personal Notes

# ** 12 **

Massage her hands. Have her sit down and close her eyes. Take off all of her jewelry. Get some lotion that smells great. Slowly and carefully take her hand in yours and rub gently. Examine every finger and rub it. Rotate the wrist slowly to release the pressure. Is she smiling? Yeah, she is. The cost of this moment of pleasure??? Nothing. Who doesn't have lotion at their disposal?

## For the female:

Remember that moments like these don't require words. If you feel the time is right, see if he wants one too. If not, remember how good it felt and save his for a special day or when he comes home stressed from his day and could use some special attention. Again, the return favor price? Free.

# Personal Notes

# ** 13 **

Don't be afraid of "that time of the month" or of the word "period." If she has a pet name for this time of the month, learn it. It happens every month to every woman. The sooner you know when her's is coming, the sooner you can look out for the mood swings and understand them. This chemical change affects each woman differently. No two are the same. Watch and learn. It could save you a lot of frustration in the long run.

## For the female:

If you know you are going through a hormonal imbalance, PMS-ing, whatever you want to call it, let him know. Take the time to explain as simply as possible what you are feeling. If you know that you begin crying for no reason the day before your period, tell him. If you know you get extra sensitive, moody or just plain bitchy, tell him. There is nothing secret about this monthly process. The more casual you make the conversation, the easier it will be for him. There is nothing worse than being an absolute witch one day and looking back the next (after your hormones have balanced) and saying, "wow... I didn't mean to say that."

## Personal Notes

honest

# ** 14 **

Be honest. Even if it hurts.

## For the female:

Listen. Even if it hurts. Be thankful he is honest. Most of all be honest yourself.

# Personal Notes

desire

# ** 15 **

If she has expressed a desire for something and you can afford it, buy it. It could be something as simple as her saying, "Wow, I love that perfume, or I haven't had German chocolate cake in years." Maybe she has something on layaway or on hold at a store. Go in and put a few dollars towards the balance she owes. Leave a little note that says you were thinking of her.

## For the female:

Always acknowledge gestures like these. Take a mental note when he is expressing his desire for something. It may be a casual reference, so pay attention. Women aren't the only ones who like presents you know.

## Personal Notes

courage

# ** 16 **

Hang a sign somewhere, that everyone will see, that expresses how you feel about her. It is okay if she is the only one who knows that the sign is for her. (Maybe you use a pet name that only she will know.) The point is that you did it. Can you just imagine how her heart will be dancing as the whole office talks about the lucky girl and the incredible man who put the sign up for her?

## For the female:

Hang a sign for him one day. On a building, in a tree, or an off-ramp from the freeway he takes every day. He will never forget it.

101 THINGS TO KNOW BEFORE YOU DATE . . .

# Personal Notes

slow

## ** 17 **

If she is more than a physical attraction, don't try to get her to have sex right away. She has been taught what you already know deep in your heart… that you really want a girl who will make you wait.

## For the female:

Think this isn't true? Go ask ten guys who are at least ten years older than the guys you are currently dating.

# Personal Notes

modest

## ** 18 **

Your penis is not a magic wand, so stop waving it like it is.

## For the female:

Men and their penis. At times, you will wonder who is in charge. It is amazing what they will do and say to satisfy their penis. Keep this in mind when a guy you barely know is telling you all those wonderful things you think you want to hear.

## Personal Notes

dignity

# ** 19 **

Leave the phrase "I told you so" out. It will save you hours of make-up if you let her be the one who says, "You were right." Pride is a very powerful thing. Start taking it away from a person and you will find yourself further and further away from the very thing you are trying to get next to.

## For the female:

Watch out for this one. I can't begin to tell you how many times you will be in a position to tell a man, "I told you so...." Don't. Be satisfied to yourself. Pride is a very important part of who and what a man is. A few minutes of personal gratification with an "I told you so...." could take months to recover from.

# Personal Notes

自信

confidence

# ** 20 **

Never short-change *you.* Let me be real clear on this. Just because you are not an athlete, doctor, lawyer, or movie star, don't think she wouldn't be interested in you. You would be surprised how many girls are just looking for the kind of guy who has most of this book mastered.

## For the female:

My only advice to you, my dear princess, is to talk to ten women who are <u>least</u> ten years older than you. Ask them how many really great, exciting, wonderful guys they knew in their lives who turned out to be nothing more than a great cover instead of a good book. They'll probably tell you a story or two about the time they judged a guy by the car he drove or the job he had. All that glitters is not gold.

101 THINGS TO KNOW BEFORE YOU DATE . . .

# Personal Notes

discover
(discovery)

# ** 21 **

Take the time to find out why she is not dating the guy she used to date. Life is too short to make all the mistakes yourself. Learn from others.

## For the female:

You don't need to give all the details, but be honest about why you no longer date someone — even if those reasons are a result of your own mistakes. Find out why his former is a former. Learn from someone else's mistakes.

# Personal Notes

## ** 22 **

Make the first date a lunch or a walk. Never a movie or a concert. How will you ever get to know her in places where you can't talk?

### For the female:

Keep the first date casual. If he asks you what you want to do, tell him. Don't say, "I don't know." Go to a place where you can talk and to get to know him. You want to know what uncomfortable means? Try being at dinner with someone, and by the time the salad arrives, you wish you were gone!

# Personal Notes

# ** 23 **

Why are you calling her if you're living with someone else? Don't you understand? If you don't have enough respect for your current girlfriend or wife, do you really expect her to believe that you are going to treat her differently?

## For the female:

Do I really need to go into this? Why would you want a guy who is lying to the woman he claims to love? (You can bet he tells her that.) No matter what the guy says (and they will come up with the most amazing lies), if he has a girl, ask yourself how you would feel if the shoe was on the other foot. There are plenty of guys out there that don't have girlfriends. If you are really attracted to him and find out that he has a girl, wait and see if he breaks up with her. If he doesn't, don't bother. Above all have self-respect.

# Personal Notes

# ** 24 **

The most intimate contact you will ever have with her will not be of a sexual nature. The touch of her hand. Her smile across the room. The look in her eyes that lets you know how special you are. Keep your eyes and heart open.

## For the female:

Remember that physical contact can be paid for. Emotional contact can't. Don't be afraid to let your feelings show with a smile, a nod, or just the touch of your hand.

# Personal Notes

compassion

# ** 25 **

Women are very different from men. There are times when we cry for no reason. When this happens, just ask if there is anything she needs to talk about. Then just hold her or stay quietly by her side. Don't say anything. Most of all don't get angry if she doesn't have an answer. No matter how silly it is to you, she may not ever have a reason she can tell you. This is just one of the many things that makes us uniquely women.

## For the female:

If he takes the time to care about why you are crying and you have a reason, tell him. Or tell him you'll talk about it later. If it's just one of those days, say "I don't have a reason, but I have to do this." He won't understand, but if he's a nice guy, he'll be there with a shoulder to cry on.

# Personal Notes

## ** 26 **

Watch twenty minutes of CNN every day so you can keep up with what she already knows.

## For the female:

Make sure you watch 20 minutes of CNN in the morning and twenty minutes before you go to sleep. You can't afford to be uninformed.

# Personal Notes

honor

# ** 27 **

You will gain so much more from a relationship when you make someone feel like they are the only thing your eyes see. It is amazing how wonderful someone will treat you when you make him or her feel like they are your whole world.

## For the female:

This goes for women too. Take my word for it. Don't ever forget it.

# Personal Notes

humble

# ** 28 **

Tone of voice is 90% of conversation. Keep that in mind every time you open your mouth, whether the situation is business or personal.

## For the female:

I can't tell you how important the tone of your voice will be in everything you do in life. You can change the course of a conversation gone bad by changing the tone of your voice. You can make a whole room stand still by the sound of your voice. You can make someone who is angry with you calm down by the tone of your voice. You can also make the hair stand up on the back of someone's neck with the tone of your voice. Listen closely and pay attention to your tone. It could save an argument or win someone's heart.

# Personal Notes

spirit

# ** 29 **

Cry if you need to. Really. She will understand and be there for you. The subject of why never has to come up unless you want it to.

## For the female:

If a man cries in your presence, you can be sure something is bothering him. Find out quickly if this something involves the two of you. If it doesn't, then ask if he wants to talk. Don't push. Let him be. Remember how many times you have been here and just let him cry. Never bring it up again unless he does. You can never tell anyone that he was crying. Crying for a man is a private thing. If you have been allowed in, keep the confidence.

# Personal Notes

partner

# ** 30 **

Don't expect her to be your mom. Those days are over. Get a life.

## For the female:

Don't do everything for him. As much as you want to be in control, make him responsible for things. You will resent him in the long run if you take on everything. One day you will grow tired of having all the responsibility and it will be too late to turn back his habit of depending on you.

101 THINGS TO KNOW BEFORE YOU DATE . . .

# Personal Notes

trust

# ** 31 **

Trust is given at first without question. It takes only seconds to ruin it and maybe never to win it back. Get the picture?

If you make a mistake, tell her. Trust in the depths of her feelings for you. Once you lie, you can't go back. If you are honest right up front, she may be angry, but she will respect you for your honesty. Then you still have a chance to repair things. The truth can be worked through. A lie cannot.

## For the female:

Trust is a hard thing to give once it has been broken. Remember to be open in your expectations of people. If you don't, they won't understand what you want from them or expect from them. Keep in mind that this works both ways. If you've broken the trust, it's a long road back, but it can be done.

## Personal Notes

acceptance

# ** 32 **

Don't be afraid if she seems smarter than you. She probably is. This is a good thing. Behind every great man is a great woman who helped him get there.

## For the female:

Never be afraid to be smart. Now this doesn't mean to throw it in a person's face every minute. Let him think he got to the end result on his own every now and then. Even if you had to give him the map.

# Personal Notes

soul

## ** 33 **

Look in her eyes when you talk to her and even more so when you are listening to her.

## For the female:

Look into his eyes when you talk to him or are listening to him. This is also a useful tool to let some one know you are NOT interested in them. Don't look them in the eye while talking. The eyes are windows to the soul. To be sure of a person and their intentions, look into their eyes.

# Personal Notes

adventure

# ** 34 **

Take her to a sporting event. You'll be surprised at what she knows. If she doesn't understand the game, grab a ball, bat, or stick and show her.

## For the female:

Take the time to watch sports on television. You can catch up on the day in sports in twenty minutes and learn something that is of interest to every guy. If you want him to be interested in your desires, take time to learn some of his.

101 THINGS TO KNOW BEFORE YOU DATE . . .

# Personal Notes

## ** 35 **

Don't be angry if she doesn't like you as much as you like her.

## For the female:

Don't ever lead a guy on for your ego or because you are trying to make someone else jealous. This is cruel and you wouldn't want it done to you. These are crazy times we live in. Let the guy know that you don't like him the way he likes you. If you can be friends, do so. If he can't get over it, stay away from him. Far away.

# Personal Notes

self-control

# ** 36 **

Never, ever, ever, ever strike her or lay a hand on her in a harmful manner. Walk away first.

## For the female:

Do not bait or push someone to the point of wanting to hit you. If the person is angry, leave. If he tries to hurt you, scream. Do not ever allow anyone to lay a hand on you that hurts. Document all physical abuse.

# Personal Notes

sensibility

## ** 37 **

Take her to the pet store and let her look at the puppies and kittens. Watch her reactions to them and most of all to your telling her she can't have one. How does she handle no?

## For the female:

Don't ask for the puppy in the window. You want every one you see. It is our nature. Buy a calendar that has pictures of baby animals if you can't resist. If you insist on being a spoiled princess, now is the time you will find out if the person you have chosen wants to put up with your nonsense.

101 THINGS TO KNOW BEFORE YOU DATE . . .

# Personal Notes

choice

# ** 38 **

Understand that no means no. The old saying that girls say yes when they really mean no is tired and thought up by men. Believe me, when she says no, she means no. Respect that; anything outside of that is rape. Plain and simple.

## For the female:

Don't tease. Remember that guys are funny creatures. A simple hug or kiss on the cheek can be misinterpreted as an invitation for more physical contact. Never be afraid to say no. Be realistic. His hotel room at two a.m.? Not a good place to talk. Save that for a breakfast or late night drink in the bar. Not his room. What did you really think he wanted when he invited you there? Conversation? No one should make you do anything you don't want to, and the way to be sure of that is to be sure of the signals you are sending. You don't have the right to tease a man or lead him on with sexual advances. There is an easy way to avoid situations that could get out of control. Don't put yourself in a position that leaves you open for trouble. This is your body. Understand that you have the power of choice and time. Use them.

# Personal Notes

delusion

# ** 39 **

Never suggest that a "baby" is the way she should express her love for you.

## For the female:

Having a child is the most difficult thing you will ever do in your life. It is a decision that requires you to examine all aspects of your own personality, your financial situation, and your future. If you have not completed your education, or you don't have a job or a direction in life you can count on by yourself, a baby is not the answer. Never allow a man to put you in a situation where you think a baby is the answer to your problems as a couple. A baby is not a game to play to get a man's attention or affection. Children are not a meal ticket. They are humans who will resent your conniving ways in the end when they realize why you had them.

101 THINGS TO KNOW BEFORE YOU DATE . . .

## Personal Notes

art

# ** 40 **

Write her a poem, a rap, a song, a letter, a paragraph or draw pictures to express your love. The back of this book has examples to get you started.

## For the female:

No matter the level of artistic quality, always remember how very special something from the heart is. Put the expression away for a later date or a great memory. If it comes from a guy that you do not feel the same for, acknowledge the uniqueness of the gesture and explain your position. Because this is such a personal thing, to continue to accept them when you don't feel the same wouldn't be fair and could land you in an uncomfortable or even dangerous situation.

101 THINGS TO KNOW BEFORE YOU DATE . . .

# Personal Notes

vigilance

## ** 41 **

Even if she is strong, understand that she needs to feel protected. The day a woman feels that you will not protect her, your relationship is on it's way to being over.

## For the female:

If you do not feel that this man would protect you and stand by you right or wrong, what are you doing with him? If this is a casual friend, then okay... anything serious requires a strong sense of security. He should know that you would stand behind him in return.

# Personal Notes

# ** 42 **

Save the "I love you" phrase until you really mean it. For the most part, guys tend to use this as a way to get into your pants. It's a worn-out phrase that is thrown around with the casualness of a pick-up basketball game at the park.

## For the female:

Watch out for this phrase. Men use it because they think it's what you want to hear. Make sure you remember the saying passed down for ages from woman to woman: actions speak louder than words.

# Personal Notes

diligent and prudent

## ** 43 **

No glove (condom), no love. Plain and simple. No excuses.

### For the female

Do I really need to go over this? Statistics of heterosexuals show that you, my princess, have the greatest chance of catching AIDS. Respect yourself. Protect yourself. Always.

101 THINGS TO KNOW BEFORE YOU DATE . . .

# Personal Notes

responsiblity

# ** 44 **

Don't think badly of her when she has her own condom for you. Respect the fact that she is informed, has a strong sense of personal perception, and respects you.

## For the female:

There is never a reason for you not to have one (condom). If you are old enough to date, you are old enough to be put in pressure situations that might get out of control. Although I would prefer that you wait until you are older and more sure of whom you are inside before you have sex, I can only guide you here. Never, ever be without a condom. Your life could depend on it.

## Personal Notes

friendship

# ** 45 **

If you decide you don't want to have a "relationship" with her, be her friend. Don't miss out on someone who could be a great friend for life.

## For the female:

Just because he doesn't like you the way you want him to doesn't mean you can't be the best of friends. I am so happy that I understood this early in life. Some of my dearest friends have been men.

101 THINGS TO KNOW BEFORE YOU DATE . . .

# Personal Notes

time

## ** 46 **

Show up on the day and near the time you say you are going to. Notice if she is ready when you get there, or at least within a respectable amount of time. (Fifteen minutes is about right.) If she constantly makes you wait for hours when you arrived when you said you would, this could be a sign of things you may not want to put up with later. Address the issue.

## For the female:

Be ready or at least within fifteen minutes of being ready when he gets there. If he is more than an hour late, and wasn't in the hospital or worse, don't go out with him. Listen to the excuse and tell him maybe you can try for another day. A guy that continuously shows up late shouldn't find you home when he does get around to coming by. Get the picture?

# Personal Notes

stability

# ** 47 **

Call when you say you are going to call. Ever call her and wonder why she has an attitude from the start of the conversation? Review the last time you spoke. When did you say you were going to call? We women are sticklers for the simple little gestures. So, do yourself a favor. Call when you say you are going to call.

## For the female:

If you are not there when he says he's going to call and he leaves a message, return the phone call. But never sit around waiting for a guy to call. Go for a walk, take a shower, go to a movie… anything. And stop picking up the phone to see if it is working. If he does this too many times, get rid of the guy. How special could you be, if he can't even call when he says he's going to?

# Personal Notes

parents

## ** 48 **

Get to know everything you can about her parents. You'll be surprised what you can learn about a person's character after listening to them talk about their parents. She will be asking you about yours, so be ready.

## For the female:

Don't be afraid to ask about his parents. This is the essence of where a human being begins. Don't be afraid to be honest about your feelings for your parents.

# Personal Notes

faith

# ** 49 **

Find out what she thinks about her faith. Does she believe in God? Allah? Buddha? Might be a good idea to find out, because she will (or should) be asking you.

## For female:

Be careful of those who claim to believe in nothing. Even that verbal gesture represents belief in something.

# Personal Notes

common sense

# ** 50 **

Never blame her for how you feel. You're responsible for your own feelings. You make the decision about how you choose to react to any given situation. Own up to that.

## For the female:

This works for you too. Accept that you control it all. I know it is hard. It is so much easier to blame someone else. "Oh, he made me miserable." No, you made yourself miserable. We have the power to choose each day how we are going to react to everything around us. It just takes a lot of practice claiming responsibility for those choices.

## Personal Notes

free will

# ** 51 **

Understand when she is going out with the girls. Every now and then she may need to see if she's still got that "vibe."

## For the female:

Go out every now and then with the girls. Women have a bad habit of getting a man and forgetting their friends. Guys don't do this; learn from them. Get the girls and go out for a walk, movie, dinner or even out dancing! Don't stop your life with your friends just because you have a guy around. Don't forget that this works both ways. To keep any kind of relationship healthy, he needs to go out with the guys now and then. Of course, this should be done in moderation on both sides.

# Personal Notes

health

# ** 52 **

I am very serious about this one. If she's gaining weight, tell her!!! Before she gains twenty pounds. And cut that crap about "Oh, you still look great." Unless she was underweight to begin with, nobody looks great with an extra twenty or thirty pounds and you know it. It is not healthy so don't patronize her. Tell her to work out or walk or something. Be willing to take an active role in this. Now this is not encouragement to put her down. Be a part of the solution. When you get ready for bed, ask her if she wants you to hold her feet while she does her crunches. If dating, suggest a jog or a trip to the gym together.

## For the female:

Can't button those jeans? Dress doesn't fit? Hey sister, you gained weight. If you were a good weight to begin with, this is not good. First off it's proven that it is not healthy. And second, you know you are not happy when you look in the mirror. Forget about pleasing the guy. You have to please yourself. If you can't walk past a mirror without cringing, or you can't walk around in underwear or some shorts without running for cover at the first sign of a human, then you need to get busy. Walking is free and is right out your front door. Don't be angry with him if he suggests in a nice way that the two of you need to do some type of physical activity together. Be happy that he cares enough to say something. Move forward and make this happen for you. Your heart and body will thank you in the long run.

# Personal Notes

happiness

# ** 53 **

Listen to her when she says she is unhappy. Take time to find out why. If they are self-involved reasons, support her. If they involve you, take this as your first hint that your relationship needs work. If you don't pay attention, she will be gone.

## For the female:

Remember that you are responsible for your own happiness. If something or someone is a part of your unhappiness, tell them. If it's something lacking in you, tell him. Keep in mind that if you are not happy with yourself, you can't make anyone else happy. The next time you find yourself sitting somewhere with your hands to your chin singing the "no body likes me song," look inside. It begins there.

# Personal Notes

discipline

# ** 54 **

No condoms. No sex. Plain and simple. No excuses. No exceptions!

## For the female:

We have been over this since you were a little girl. Don't be swayed by the heat of the moment. The gift of physical contact is the most precious thing you can share with someone. Have respect for yourself. Would you let just anyone off the street wear your favorite outfit or borrow your new car? Then why give your soul to a stranger? If you always make sure you are protected, you have made the choice about how you are going to approach your adult life. How many people do you need to see die? AIDS is no joke. It's real and it can happen to the nicest people. I don't want to bury my daughter or son because they let one moment of emotion change the course of their life.

# Personal Notes

forgiveness

# ** 55 **

If you have cheated and been caught, do everything you can think of to win her trust back. No matter how long the list is, or how often the same thing is repeated. Eventually we can forgive. The worst answer to "why?" is "I don't know why." Better figure it out, brother. A large part of the healing process is understanding the why. Then ask her what she needs you to do to help her believe in you again. This is assuming she has decided to give your relationship and you a second chance.

## For the female:

This is a hard one. I wish I could say that, if the guy cheats on you, get rid of him. This does not always work in every situation. Every relationship is unique and must be looked at as such. Don't base your actions on what your girlfriends tell you they would do if they were in the same situation. No one knows what they would do in this predicament until it happens. You have to weigh the situation and decide for yourself. What are the circumstances? Do you believe him? Can you trust him again? One thing I can tell you for sure. If a man does it repeatedly, he does not care for you. He has a problem. You should get away from him as fast as you can because he will only bring you pain. He does not respect himself. He has no self-worth. Leave him alone before he drags you down with him.

101 THINGS TO KNOW BEFORE YOU DATE . . .

## Personal Notes

# ** 56 **

<u>Gift</u>: That which is voluntarily bestowed (given) without expectations of return or compensation.

That means that the gift you give belongs to her. Don't be an ass and ask for it back or take it back.

## For the female:

Remember to be careful what you ask for—you might get it. Never argue with a man who wants something back. Give it to him and never speak to him again. When you give a gift, realize it is just that. Don't ever ask for it back. Don't give gifts unless you are sure you don't ever want it back. So, in other words, don't give away something that is precious and dear to you. The guy may be gone one day, but your memories of the precious items you no longer have won't be.

101 THINGS TO KNOW BEFORE YOU DATE . . .

## Personal Notes

silence

# ** 57 **

Having a horrible day with her that is getting progressively worse every time you open your mouth? Shut up, stop, leave, walk outside and re-enter like none of it ever happened. Like you just arrived. It may not always work, but nine times out of ten it will change the momentum of negativity.

## For the female:

Just can't seem to stop a bad situation from spiraling into a hole? Stop talking and change the environment. You may find yourselves laughing at the whole thing. If not, one of you should leave and try talking later. Sometimes there isn't any other choice.

# Personal Notes

dream

# ** 58 **

No matter how silly or unrealistic her dreams may be, support her. She'll eventually figure out if her dream is not for her. Your support, however, will win a place in her heart forever.

## For the female:

Don't be shy about what you dream about. You can't expect someone to support your dreams if you never tell them what they are.

101 THINGS TO KNOW BEFORE YOU DATE . . .

# Personal Notes

pain

# ** 59 **

If you've had too much to drink, don't start a deep conversation. Words or actions based in alcohol mean nothing.

## For the female:

If you find yourself in this situation more than once (once could be un-intentional), you have to seriously examine what is wrong inside. Few people hide behind liquor or drugs without serious personal issues.

101 THINGS TO KNOW BEFORE YOU DATE . . .

# Personal Notes

cherish

# ** 60 **

Treat her like she is a princess and I guarantee you'll be treated like a prince.

## For the female:

There is no greater feeling than that of being cherished. Respect it, relish it, and return it.

101 THINGS TO KNOW BEFORE YOU DATE . . .

## Personal Notes

relaxed

# ** 61 **

Allow her to exhale without fear. This means allowing her time to be without her guards. No matter what she says, she doesn't always want to be strong. Take the reigns and make all the choices once in a while. Let her sit back without making any decisions or running anything for a few hours. Every now and then she may want you to be in control of everything.

## For the female:

Exhaling means letting go. Forgetting all the fears and worries. Letting go of control and just letting the moment be what it is. Let him make all the choices for you for an hour. This freedom is so liberating mentally. Let him feel like the boss, even if he makes mistakes.

## Personal Notes

# ** 62 **

Pretend to yourself that she would break if you dropped her. If you always keep that in the back of your mind no matter what, you will be okay.

## For the female:

No matter how tough you try to be, don't forget to be a lady.

101 THINGS TO KNOW BEFORE YOU DATE . . .

# Personal Notes

# ** 63 **

Let her feel secure and safe no matter what, even if you are in an argument. Don't ever let your invisible arms around her drop. Ever.

## For the female:

Let him feel that he is your protector, even if you know you can take care of yourself.

101 THINGS TO KNOW BEFORE YOU DATE . . .

## Personal Notes

cleanup

# ** 64 **

Look in her refrigerator. What a person eats, how clean they keep their surrounding, tells you a lot about them.

## For the female:

Check out his refrigerator. Give him a small break for being a man, but look. If you see mold, watch out, he may be looking for a mommy.

101 THINGS TO KNOW BEFORE YOU DATE . . .

# Personal Notes

# ** 65 **

Now, about that bathroom. If it's not clean and there are dirty towels and clothes everywhere, what does this say about her? Okay, maybe she was in a hurry that morning, but how does the rest of the house look? What about her kitchen? Does her place look lived in or a disaster? What is her reaction to the way her place looks?

## For the female:

Look at his bathroom. If it is a mess with urine stains all over the seat, hair, towels, and dirty clothes everywhere, and he knew you were coming by… this should tell you something. Perhaps that he doesn't think much of himself or you. Again, you might be dealing with someone looking for a mommy. Now let's get to your house. If you knew he was coming, why is it a mess? If you don't have time, get a service. Once a month spring for someone to come and do what you can't seem to get done. No harm in that, just do it. If you are that busy working, you can afford a cleaning person once in a while. Ask your friends. Someone will know someone who does this for a living. Don't pretend that you aren't getting any help. How are you going to explain the need for this wonderful service should the two of you get together? Hey, then you can split the cost!

# Personal Notes

danger

# ** 66 **

Never, ever, ever, ever, give her anything to ingest (that means eat or drink) without her knowledge.

## For the female:

Until you know a guy real well, watch yourself and what he gives you to eat or drink. These are crazy times we live in. This is why you always, and I mean always, let someone know where you are, who you are with and when you are expected back. Know a guy's full name and address before you leave with him. Look at his driver's license. Anyone who has a problem with showing you stuff like this is the kind of guy you don't want to be around. Know the kind of car he drives. Make a point to notice the license plate. Let someone know this information. Think I am kidding? Look on a milk carton. Those aren't just kids' faces there, you know.

# Personal Notes

obligation

# ** 67 **

Call when you say you are going to call. Has someone explained that "later" means the same day? Not a few days or weeks later. This is probably the hardest thing for guys to learn. When you say, "I'll call you later," we think you mean today. Later today. A better way to put it would be, "I'll call you later, if I get time." Or "I'll call you this week." Make sure you do. Understand that men and women are very different. Words do not mean to you what they mean to us. Think of it like this: If your best friend called and said hey, let's play ball later, when would you be expecting to play?

## For the female:

This works both ways. If you are having a hard time getting someone to understand this, sit down and explain it to them. Point out exact days and times. You must also understand that most of the time, the lack of follow-through is not done with malice. Men don't understand that it matters when they say they will call later and that call comes a day or a week later.... Often it works to make a joke out of it. If you get a guy who says he will call right back and calls you the next day, start the conversation off with a laugh and say, "I'm glad I didn't need bail..." or "I am sure glad I wasn't stranded with a flat, I'd still be there waiting for you to call back" and laugh. It's all you really can do.

# Personal Notes

# ** 68 **

Standing by her side does not mean to do so with silent support. If you disagree with her, or think she is heading down the wrong path, tell her softly.

Example: "I think you are missing a chance at something you are really good at, but if this is what you truly want, I will support you 100%. Could we talk about this a little more?"

## For the female:

Don't be angry if he does not agree with your every move. A real friend doesn't. The last thing you need is someone who tells you that you're right all the time. You aren't.

# Personal Notes

farewell

# ** 69 **

If you decide she is not the girl for you, tell her. She is not going to fall apart. Don't drag it out. Nothing is worse than letting a relationship go until there is nothing left but anger and hate. If she is the kind of girl who falls apart and becomes violent, don't hesitate to call the local authorities and file the necessary paperwork. Women can be as dangerous as men. Never forget this.

## For the female:

If the guy tells you it's over, let him go. Of course it hurts. Of course you don't want to believe that he is serious. He is. Don't call his house and hang up. Don't find reasons to bump into him. Do not stalk him, leave him crying messages, follow him, or bother his new interest. Get over it. Go ahead and cry. Then pick up the phone and call your best girlfriend. She will probably be able to give you ten reasons why it's a good thing he's gone. Remember this: "Rejection is God's protection."

101 THINGS TO KNOW BEFORE YOU DATE . . .

# Personal Notes

## ** 70 **

If you ask her "what's wrong? and she says "nothing," really pay attention. Did she look away (usually a sign that she really wants to talk) or did she look you directly in the eye (a direct indication that she does not want to discuss the matter)? This body language is a good indicator. Sometimes what we really want is to tell you what is wrong with us, but we are not sure how to say it. Look for the signs. They usually aren't hard to read once you know them.

## For the female:

Okay, you and I both know we women are good for this one. So if he takes the time to ask you what's wrong, don't keep saying "nothing" if it really is something. Play that game too often and he will stop asking.

101 THINGS TO KNOW BEFORE YOU DATE . . .

# Personal Notes

reliable

## ** 71 **

Call when you say you're going to call. No matter where you are, no matter how far. Even if you only have time to say, "I can't talk." I can't tell you how many women you will knock off their feet if you can master this. A simple "Hi, I know I said I would call, but I am in the middle of something and I wanted to make sure you knew I remembered" will win the heart of the most difficult woman.

## For the female:

This is the lesson that overwhelmingly came up as the most common complaint women have against men. That's why I have repeated it so many times in this book. It may take a while to teach him this one. Pay attention to effort, and <u>lack</u> of effort.

101 THINGS TO KNOW BEFORE YOU DATE . . .

## Personal Notes

self-defense

# ** 72 **

No condom. No sex. No love. Have you ever heard of AIDS? Do you know the current statistics? (See the end of the book if you need to be informed.) One moment of haste can seal your fate. Forever.

## For the female:
Carry a condom in your purse. Don't ever tell yourself that this one time won't matter. It could be the one time that costs you your life. Are you willing to pay the price?

# Personal Notes

respect

# ** 73 **

Unless you've agreed in advance, don't drop by without calling. Not because she might be busy, but because you need to respect her space. Call first. Remember, surprises aren't always fun.

## For the female:

Respect goes both ways here. Don't drop by without calling or getting the okay to do so ahead of time. You might not like what you find. Or, you may catch him sleeping and he may not be happy you woke him up. Just call and save yourself the trouble. Demand the same respect in return. What if you just put your mask on your face... popped your favorite movie in... and sat down to do some paperwork... is this really the time you want to be interrupted?

# Personal Notes

opportunity

## ** 74 **

If you have something to say, then say it. There is nothing worse than wishing you had said something, didn't, and are now sitting there looking back saying "If I coulda, woulda, shoulda." The old saying "live each day like it is your last" may seem odd when you are young, but ask yourself this: If your wife or girlfriend goes off to work and you never see them again, would your last words have been what you wanted them to be?

## For the female:

No matter how hard, say what you have to say. Some of the most painful memories are situations where you wish you had said how you felt and didn't. There aren't many things that will nag at you in life like looking back at a missed opportunity that is gone forever.

# Personal Notes

親和力
affinity

# ** 75 **

Pick up the phone and call her for no reason. Just let her know that she was passing through your mind. You don't need to say anything else. A simple "hello" and "I was thinking of you" carries all the magic in the world.

## For the female:

When you have a guy that does this, be happy, very happy. Don't forget to return the gesture. If he is at work and doesn't like calls there, e-mail a hello to let him know he crossed your mind. Call his home phone or cell and leave a message that just says, I was thinking of you today. The results are priceless.

# Personal Notes

## ** 76 **

Remember that you can't judge a book by its cover. Ever got a present that was wrapped really pretty, but when opened, it wasn't what you hoped for? Take your time. Don't be influenced by your peers to go after a girl based on her looks.

## For the female:

Great looking guys do not automatically mean great boyfriends. The kind of man he is on the inside far outweighs what he looks like on the outside. If something about him has caught your interest, take the time to find out who he is inside. Haven't you ever looked at a couple and thought to yourself, I wonder what she saw in him? She took the time to look inside.

# Personal Notes

我愛你

I love you

# ** 77 **

Just because you say "I love you" doesn't mean she has to say it back. Don't sit there looking at her like she is missing an eye. Know that if it is returned out of trained response instead of true meaning, you could have problems later.

## For the female:

Now here's an uncomfortable situation. All of a sudden the guy you are dating says, "I love you" and then "Uh, didn't you hear me? I said I love you." If this happens and you don't feel the same way, you do not have to say it back to make someone feel good or to get out of an uncomfortable moment. A "Yes, I heard you. That really made me smile" will be a great place to start. You may want to lead into why you don't feel the same way.

# Personal Notes

natural

# ** 78 **

Be yourself. Not what you think she wants. Trying to be anything other than who you are always, and I mean always, backfires.

## For the female:

Be yourself. Not what you think he wants or tells you to be. If you really don't like football, don't let him believe you do, get together and then nag every Sunday when he watches the game. If you don't like cigarette smoke, don't say it's okay and then argue every time he lights up. It is safer to simply be who you are. You'll never have a problem remembering that. It's great that he loves your long hair and tight rear end, but if it's not all yours, best to let him know in advance.

# Personal Notes

conflict

## ** 79 **

If she drops by, don't take personal calls from other women. Unless of course the message you are trying to send is that you don't care for or respect her.

## For the female:

If you come over to see a man and he gets a phone call from another women that appears quite personal, leave. He should have enough respect to ask her to call later. If the call is business or school-related, he should stop, explain that he needs to take this call for a moment, and be done with it.

## Personal Notes

observation

# ** 80 **

Watch how she treats the people in her life. Family, friends, the waiter in the restaurant. This will tell you a lot about her as a person. Is she wonderful to you and a rabid cat to the waiter, other women, strangers? Most of the warning signs to people are obvious from the beginning. You just need to keep your eyes open.

## For the female:

Keep an eye out for these things. You want to know about the guy? Watch how he treats other people. Looking at him, it will become obvious when he is sweet as pie to you and then bites the waitress' head off. He opens your door and then lets it slam in the face of the old woman walking behind you? Don't miss these obvious signs. The same holds true for you. Putting on airs won't last long, my dear. Sooner or later your true colors will show. Why not make them beautiful?

101 THINGS TO KNOW BEFORE YOU DATE . . .

# Personal Notes

quiet

# ** 81 **

Invite her to spend the afternoon reading. You read what you want, she reads what she wants. Just be together. No words necessary. Times like this will be priceless. Watch how she behaves with quiet time.

## For the female:

Invite him over for quiet time. See if he can sit still for a couple of hours, just enjoying your presence. If you find someone to spend time with like this, enjoy the moments. They are priceless and hard to find. He can't sit still? What does this tell you about him?

## Personal Notes

effort

# ** 82 **

If you ask her where she would like to go on a date and she tells you, try to make it happen. If you can't do every part of the dream date, try for one or two aspects of it. Don't get angry if it's not what you really want to do. If you had something in mind, you shouldn't have asked.

## For the female:

One of the most annoying answers in the world is "I don't know." If you get the chance and some one says, what do you want to do, have an answer ready!!! There won't be many chances in life when you get asked what you alone would like to do, so take advantage of the times when it's offered. Don't be offended if he could only make certain things come true for you. It is the thought and effort that count.

# Personal Notes

# ** 83 **

Come up with ideas of your own for a date. Be spontaneous. Be creative. Have the whole evening planned from start to finish. Call her up and say, "Be ready at eight." You should give her an idea of what to wear, so that she is not over or under dressed.

## For the female:

Go along with his plans. Try new things. Be ready with ideas of your own. No matter how silly the idea is, give it a try unless it makes you uncomfortable in some way. He went to all that trouble to bring you dinner at the office, so the two of you could tailgate together. Enjoy a man that goes to this much trouble for you.

# Personal Notes

unusual

# ** 84 **

Flowers are common. Men send them without much thought attached. If you must send them, do it when it's not expected. Be creative, send something unusual. Spend time figuring out what would let her know this moment was premeditated, not a knee-jerk response from a commercial you saw or an ad you read.

## For the female:

Send him flowers. Most men never get them. Especially on an ordinary day, for no reason. It's a wonderful surprise that lets him know that you don't expect all the getting without doing some of the giving.

## Personal Notes

important

# ** 85 **

Call when you say you're going to call. Call collect. E-mail. Borrow a phone. Do whatever you have to. Just call. Get it?

## For the female:

If he hasn't got this by now, leave notes everywhere. Or you can try this . . . don't be there when he does call.

# Personal Notes

# ** 86 **

Find out what she dreams of doing or becoming. Listen to her as she expresses desires for the future. Periodically ask her how she's coming on them. Often we get so caught up in our day-to-day obligations that we forget our dreams or those of the people around us. Remind her that she should pursue them.

## For the female:

Don't get so caught up in pushing and supporting everyone else (especially the man in your life) that you forget your own dreams. It is a major part of who you are, so don't set them aside for long. Take that step. Go back to school and finish. Write that book. Take the first step and the rest will follow. You will be so glad you did. It's almost a guarantee that you will hold it against everyone when it is really your own fault if you don't pursue them. Remember that it is okay to put <u>you</u> first sometimes.

# Personal Notes

encourage

# ** 87 **

Hold her feet while she does her crunches. Go with her on a jog or a power walk. Teach her how to shadow-box twenty minutes a day. Women need to be encouraged and sometimes pushed in these areas.

## For the female:

Don't take it wrong if he says "let's go for a walk" or "do you want me to hold your feet while you do your sit-ups?" Be happy that he wants to be a part of your life like that. If he doesn't seem interested in joining in with you, how interested is he in the other things in your life? Time for a review of him and yourself. Just what are you settling for?

# Personal Notes

history

# ** 88 **

Don't lie to her about your past or conveniently leave out touchy details. If you have children, an ex-wife, psychotic ex-girlfriend, permanent sexual disease, or incurable social problems, let her be the one to decide if she can handle it.

## For the females:

If he is honest and tells you up-front about something serious, take your time deciding if you can handle it. If he waits too long to tell you important secrets about his life, you must look at this closely. Why would he leave out such important details and, more importantly, what else has he "forgotten" to tell you?

# Personal Notes

sexual intercourse

# ** 89 **

Don't lie about sexual activity. You have no right to play Russian roulette with her life. Be a man not a punk. She has the right to know if you are sleeping with other people, so she can decide for herself and protect herself. Don't lie. You don't have the right.

## For the female:

This is one of the most important things you must know in a relationship. If you find out a guy is lying to you, he will probably lie again. You have to begin to ask yourself questions about how dangerous you want to lead your life. Be honest with yourself and your partner. You do not have the right to play with anyone's life either.

# 101 THINGS TO KNOW BEFORE YOU DATE . . .

## Personal Notes

passion

# ** 90 **

Should the relationship progress to a union that involves physical contact remember that love can be soft, beautiful, passionate, fulfilling and memorable. It is a unique expression of feelings. It can also be nothing more than atoms and energy erratically bouncing off one another. The choice is one you should make together.

## For the female:

There will be moments in your life that the physical contact you share with another person will be so wonderful it will bring you to tears. There will also be times when it will be nothing more than frantic passion that leaves you breathless and sweating. Understand and know the difference. Strive to find someone with whom you can share both ends of the spectrum.

# Personal Notes

question

# ** 91**

Closed mouths don't get fed. If you want to know something, ask her, write it down, or e-mail it. Don't ever stop seeing someone without at least giving him or her the courtesy of telling them why. A simple note or message on an answering machine will do.

## For female:

Stop sitting there trying to figure out if he loves me, he loves me not. If you want to know, be a woman and ask. If that is not comfortable or convenient, e-mail him or write him a note. Just be sure you really want to know the answer.

# Personal Notes

keep promises

# ** 92 **

Don't make promises you can't keep. We women have a funny way of remembering every last one of them in detail. For years.

## For females:

Too many broken promises are the sign of a man who talks a good talk but doesn't follow through and someone to get rid of. Don't make promises you have no intention of keeping.

# Personal Notes

comfortable

# ** 93 **

Don't ever make her feel silly for trying something out of character or bold. Laugh with her, not at her. Women and their egos are fragile things. Once we feel we have been laughed at, it may take forever to build up the nerve to be adventurous again.

## For the female:

Be daring. Do something out of character once in a while. If it doesn't work, laugh with him or at yourself. Don't be afraid to try again. Use your imagination and go for it. Spice is the key to life. Use it.

# Personal Notes

reaction

# ** 94 **

Watch some silly love stories with her and pay attention. There is a reason why she watches a particular movie. Does she watch it every month? Only when she's mad at you? Only when she's feeling blue? You don't need to ask her anything. Watch her reactions to the scenes. You could learn something. It could give you ideas when you are trying to think of something romantic to do for her. Rent that movie yourself and watch the scene (over and over) that made her get that certain smile on her face. There are way too many options available for ideas. Use them.

## For the female:

Watch some "chic flicks" with him. This could give you an idea of what kind of romantic he is or isn't; what he thinks is silly and maybe why. It is also the best time to bring up some things you would like to see him do, with the example right in front of him. If you just can't get him to understand what you mean by suggesting a certain thing, find a scene in movie, book, video, or magazine article and hand it to him. It might be a good idea if you watched his reaction in these movies as well. Comments like, "Wow, that only happens in the movies," could be a signal of something you could work on yourself.

101 THINGS TO KNOW BEFORE YOU DATE . . .

## Personal Notes

family

# ** 95 **

What are the names of her family members? Ask about them from time to time. Understanding her relationship with them could help you understand her. It could explain mood swings associated with phone calls from a certain family member. If you plan on keeping her around, this is a must.

## For the female

Make sure you ask questions about his family and his relationship with them. It might explain his feelings about holidays, birthdays or other events. Does mom call him every day with things for him to do? Do other family members depend on him for everything? These are things you want to know in advance. This is especially crucial with regard to children, should he have any. What is the relationship with the mother? Does he get calls at all hours of the day and night for ridiculous things? Do his friends just stop by without calling and stay till the wee hours of the morning? Better find out about all the people in his life before you get too involved.

# Personal Notes

你覺得怎樣

what do you think?

# ** 96 **

What are her views on the current state of the world? Have some yourself. Over dinner would be a great place to bring up casual conversation about current events. Do you want a woman that doesn't know anything about the world around her?

## For the female:

Make sure you have an opinion about what is going on in the world. No man wants a woman who can only tell him what is on sale as Bloomingdale's. Get on-line and get the daily news in one e-mail. There should never be a day when you have nothing to talk about—even if it is just the weather, the cycle of the moon, the location of Mars. Be interesting. Be informed. Be ready to learn.

# Personal Notes

孩子

children

# ** 97 **

What are her views on contraception and abortion? Know your position and be prepared to defend it. If you are not interested in having children or being in a relationship that could leave you tied to someone for years, you should be up front with her. Ultimately you must understand that if you involve yourself in a relationship that includes intimate contact, and you are not protected, you must accept responsibility for your actions. Don't want kids? Stop having sex with everyone you see.

## For the female:

Make sure you know exactly how you feel about the topics of children and contraception. If your desire is to have a child and his isn't, then know this from the beginning. Respect his position. Children are not tools to get money or a man. Don't ever think that love will come after the baby is born. It won't. Do you really want to look in the face of a child fifteen years down the road and tell them that their father was a one-night stand you really didn't know? Or that he never wanted kids but you had one anyway? Children are not a board game to get the "sit at home and wait for the check" ticket. If you decide to have children, be prepared to be a mother. Children are a direct reflection of their immediate caregiver. If you don't have a job, an education, a trade, or civic interests, just what do you think your children are going to grow up to be?

101 THINGS TO KNOW BEFORE YOU DATE . . .

# Personal Notes

favorite

# ** 98 **

What are her favorite foods? What are her favorite colors? Take the time to find out. It could save you time and money when you go to buy her a gift. Most of all know yours.

## For the female:

Make sure you take the time to find out simple things about a guy. What does he like to eat? Is there a color he loves? You will soon see that it is the simple things in life that make all the difference in the world. A small gift during a particular sports season that has his favorite team colors or logo will be cherished for years.

# Personal Notes

# ** 99 **

What does feeling safe mean to her? You have to know the answer to this. What are her pet peeves? Does she have any allergies? What are the happiest memories in her life? What are the saddest memories in her life?

## For the female:

You should have no problem answering those questions. They are the core of who you are. Be ready to give them to anyone you are contemplating a serious relationship with. It would be a good idea to know the same about him. Don't think for one minute that there isn't something out there that worries him. Take the time to find out.

# Personal Notes

# ** 100 **

If you haven't bothered to find out the answer to the basic questions in this book by the time you are contemplating a serious relationship with her, consider yourself history. I thought you wanted a relationship built on a solid foundation this time. Get to memorizing. There are only 101 things in this book. I repeated the more difficult topics to help out.

## For the female:

If he hasn't bothered to get the answer to these basic questions, get rid of him. He is shallow, and probably after only one thing. Is that what you are really looking for? Get to memorizing, girlfriend. There are only 101 things in this book. They affect you as much as the man you are planning to date, love, and cherish. Be the very best that you can be and you will attract the very best. Like attracts like. Never forget it.

## Personal Notes

conclusion

# ** 101 **

Understand that you are a dessert, not the main course. You're a luxury not a necessity. She's complete with you and complete without you. Once you understand this, you will find a much healthier relationship.

## For the female:

No need to repeat this one. You are a special precious being. You are a woman, a lady, a princess, a warrior, a creator, a mother, a leader, and the source of strength for a family unit. No one sits above you on this earth unless you lower yourself. Don't ever forget it.

Oh,

One last thing,

CALL WHEN
YOU SAY YOU
ARE GOING TO
CALL!!!!!!!!!!!

# Personal Notes

# SAMPLE DATE LOCATIONS

- A park bench
- A museum
- The zoo
- Get a local city guide; go all over the city and explore it together like tourists
- The beach or fountain if the beach is miles away
- Go hiking
- A spot somewhere up high to watch the sunset
- Your house for an afternoon of her favorite movies
- The bookstore
- Somewhere you can see the stars. A remote area without a lot of lights or an observatory. Most cities have one. Make sure you know a couple of constellations.
- The park
- The Zoo
- Go-cart racing
- Bowling

# SAMPLE CONVERSATION TOPICS

- Do you vote? Why or why not?

- Do you believe in God? Why or why not?

- Why do you think girls like love stories so much?

- Are you afraid of anything?

- What's really behind the destruction of the American family? Or is everything fine?

- If you could be guaranteed one wish, what would it be?

- Can you separate religion and politics?

- Best joke you ever heard?

- Most embarrassing moment?

- The best thing you remember about childhood?

- The worst thing you remember about high school?

- The most romantic thing you have ever heard?

- Your dream vacation?

- If you did not have to worry about money, what would you want to do for a living?

- What do you want to be five years from now? Ten?

- Most important thing you learned from your mom?

- Your dad?

- Do you believe in miracles?

- Is there such a thing as fate or are we masters of or own destiny?

- If you could write a book about something, what would it be?

- If you couldn't say the words "I love you" and you only had one chance, how would you let a person know that you loved them?

- If you could meet anyone dead or alive, who would it be and why?

- Can women do anything men can do?

- Is there such a thing as extra-sensory perception?

- Do women have a sixth sense men don't have?

# Personal Notes

# SAMPLE MENUS

## DELI SANDWICH, CHIPS, SODA OR $H_2O$

This can be bought at your local grocery store or even corner gas station if you are in a bind… Ask her friends what her favorite snacks are and make it like a picnic.

## FINGER FOODS

Fresh fruit, caramel dip, nuts, raisins, cool whip, cheese crackers, carrot sticks, and some ranch dressing. Top it off with a nice glass of white zinfandel if you are of age or great combo juices like mango peach. Throw in some melted chocolate if you are really daring. All available at your local grocery store.

## SOUP AND SANDWICH

Never under estimate the power of a childhood memory. Everybody loves soup. If you are a great cook, make some from scratch. If not, there are plenty of great canned and frozen soups that taste great. Dress it up with a great sandwich or crackers. Here's where a nice dessert can put a great ending to a simple meal. There are plenty of pre-made desserts in the frozen food section. Be sure to read all directions, no matter how simple that may seem. Some soups are better with milk than water. Some don't require adding anything. Read the directions.

# STEAK AND SALAD

You can get an inexpensive piece of meat and buy a package of marinade to make it taste like it cost a lot more. Look for rib eye if you are on a tight budget. You can pick up two for about six dollars. If you are on a medium budget, buy a T-bone. If you've got some bucks to spend, buy a porterhouse or filet mignon. Marinades are found in the pre-mixed seasoning section usually on the same aisle as the salad dressing. Might as well pick up some salad dressing while you are in the aisle. Ranch dressing or a nice balsamic vinaigrette is always a safe choice. Marinate your meat for at least an hour. Pierce the meat with a fork. (Stab the piece of meat and make a bunch of little holes in it.) Salad can be bought pre-made in the vegetable section. Broil your steak in the oven or cook in a pan on top of the stove if you don't have a broiler. You must watch your meat very closely as it does not take long to cook a steak. Especially if it is thin. When the meat gets brown, turn it over. Cut a small hole in the center of the steak. If it is bright pink, let it cook longer. Open your salad to let it breathe. Shake it out into a large bowl and put it in the refrigerator until you are ready to serve. If you have the cash, grab a loaf of garlic bread that can be heated up and served. Directions are usually on the bag.

# TACOS

One half pound ground beef or turkey or chicken
Pre-packaged seasoning for tacos
One small onion. Optional
Small pan

Brown the meat on medium high. This means cook it until the red goes away. Add your seasonings, onion (if you are using one), and a half-cup of water (if you don't have a measuring cup, measure two fingers in a drinking glass). You can also add some salsa if you have some (about three spoonfuls). Keep cooking until everything is mixed. Turn the heat down to low and let simmer. This means let it sit, occasionally opening the top and stirring. Unless you are really adventurous, save yourself the aggravation and get the preformed taco shells. Heat them in the oven on 300 for about three minutes. Or in the microwave for 40 seconds. Leave the oven on for reuse. Take your meat and spoon it into the shells. Top off with cheese and put in the oven or micro until melted. Have a small bowl of lettuce and one of tomatoes, so that she can add more toppings. Sour cream is also a nice touch. If this all sounds too challenging, look for the most authentic Mexican restaurant you can find and order take out. Put it on a plate from home. Make sure you tell her that you didn't cook it because she may ask you for the recipe.

# GARLIC CHICKEN

Depending on your budget (buy what you can afford):
Boneless breasts, legs, thighs, it does not matter
One garlic clove (found in the vegetable and fruit section)
One small onion
One half-cup olive oil

Get a medium-sized frying pan. Place your oil, garlic, and onion in the pan. Lightly brown. Add your chicken. At this point you can do a number of sauces depending on taste. A can of mushroom or tomato basil soup over the top of the chicken will work. Cover and let simmer on low for an hour. Test your meat by sticking a fork in it. It should be tender and pull easily from the bone. It will not hurt for the chicken to sit on very low until you are ready to serve. Instant rice, potatoes, or pasta is a good combo with this chicken. A nice salad always tops off any meal.

JOSEFA SALINAS

# SAMPLE LOVE NOTES

My restless heart skipped a beat
as I took your hand in mine.
How do I let you know
that as I look into your eyes, I cease to breathe?
My heart
full of your essence
pounds wildly in my chest.
Alone at night,
I remember your face
my soul sleeps with angels.

You have made the caterpillar inside of me
bloom into a butterfly with wings.
Blood races through my veins
looking for a place to stop
and cannot find one.
My heart beats faster
at the thought of you within its reach.
I close my eyes
and I can feel your breath on the back of my neck
searching for a place to mingle with mine.
I slowly turn,
my eyes searching,
only to find an empty room.
How I miss you.

As I sit close,
you rest your head on my shoulder
and I dream of kissing your face.
First one cheek,
then the other.
I want to smother your lips
and take your breath as my own.
I long to wrap my body tightly within yours
and search for the look I know
lays deep within the soul of your captivating eyes.
But no,
this is different.
This is more.
This is worth waiting for.
This is worth learning.
How could I explore your body
when I have not discovered the magic of your smile?

♥

Anticipating your eyes
Remembering your smile
Softly your hand in mine
Slowly I close my eyes
I can smell you near
Beginnings are wonderful.

## JOSEFA SALINAS

Our eyes met across the room
And it seemed as though I could hear time stand still
I required no air
My heart did not beat
In seconds
Your smile imprinted my soul
Years have passed since that day
Although our lips have never met
The memory of that moment flutters in my heart.

Come with me and let me show you
the light that dances just beyond the moon.
Dream with me of days to come
and mountains yet to climb.
Fill me with all that is yours,
I shall engulf you with all that is mine.

# NATIONAL HOTLINE NUMBERS

National Respite Locator Service: 1-800-773-5433

Rape and Abuse National Network:1-800-656-4673

National Domestic Violence Hotline: 1-800-799-7233

Youth Crisis Hotline: 1-800-448-4663

Child Find America: 1-800-292-9688

National Runaway Switchboard: 1-800-621-4000

National Victim Center: 1-800-394-2255

PAX: 1-866-SPEAKUP

Project Cuddle:  1-888-628-3353

Breast Cancer Awareness: 1-888-833-6473

Fair Community Lending Services: 1-888-908- DOOR

# HIV/AIDS STATISTICS

As of the end of 2004, an estimated 40 million people worldwide—37 million adults and 2.5 million children younger than 15 years—were living with HIV/AIDS.

An estimated 5 million new HIV infections occured worldwide during 2003; that is about 14,000 infections each day.

In 2003, approximately 2,000 children under the age of 15 years, and 6,000 young people aged 15 to 24 years became infected with HIV every day.

In 2003 alone, HIV/AIDS-associated illnesses caused the deaths of approximately 3 million people worldwide, including an estimated 500,000 children younger than 15 years.

The Centers for Disease Control and Prevention (CDC) estimate that 850,000 to 950,000 U.S. residents are living with HIV infection, one-quarter of whom are unaware of their infection.

Of new infections among women in the United States, CDC estimates that approximately 75 percent of the women were infected through heterosexual sex and 25 percent through injection drug use.

Information provided by U.S. Department of Health and Human services
www.niaid.nih.gov

# PAY IT FORWARD

After watching the movie "Pay it Forward" (Warner Brothers, October 2000) I was moved by the spirit of its theme. This is for you, my friends. I hope that if given the chance, you will do it for someone coming along the path with you. Remember the hand that pulled you up by reaching for someone be-hind you.

# bel.

they call me bel.

i am an artist and i love creating -
be it in the form of graphic design,
poetry, song, dance, drawing,
photography, or simply writing
in my journal.

thank you to my family - dad, mom,,
gery - i miss you everyday. thank you
to dave - DreamReal and one three eight
are the next graphic design monsters -
lookout world, here we come!
and to josefa, thank you couldn't even begin to describe
what i want to say for the opportunities
you have given me - on to the next project!

cover design by: annabellayug@hotmail.com

# Proceeds from the sale of every book will be distributed as follows:

### $1.00 Heritage Begins Within
to assist single mothers in home ownership
and secondary education scholarships.
www.101thingstoknow.com & www.fcls123.com

### $.50 Barbara Davis Center for Childhood Diabetes.
www.barbaradaviscenter.org

### $.25 Breast cancer research
www.thedeniserobertsfoundation.org

### $.25 to Hope for Life
for the continuation of Community Day
www.communityday.net

### $.25 Knowledge is Power
in 1993 Josefa started this foundation for Power 106 in Los
Angeles. She applauds their continued efforts.

# ABOUT THE AUTHOR

Known as the Southland's "Angelita de la Noche," Josefa's silky smooth yet commanding voice has delighted listeners up and down the coast for twenty years. This breakthrough female Latina personality has become a role model for women and a powerful symbol for Latinas. After studying psychology and political science at the University of Michigan, Josefa worked in juvenile probation, but felt the need to use more of her talents. She held down broadcasting positions in Talk, Jazz/Newage, Hip Hop, Urban AC, Urban, and Crossover formats. She has become a powerful and respected community leader and champion for the underserved. As a manager, she has successfully shaped the careers of many artists and producers, most notably Grammy award winner Coolio. Josefa divides her time between radio, writing, and raising her seven-year-old son.